JAN 1 3 2016

Gr 3-6

D0787458

JAN 3 2019

OUR
GRE★T
STATES

WHAT'S GREAT ABOUT
SOUTH DAKOTA?

* Mary Meinking

LERNER PUBLICATIONS * MINNEAPOLIS

CONTENTS

SOUTH DAKOTA
WELCOMES YOU! ✳ 4

Copyright © 2015
by Lerner Publishing Group, Inc.

Content Consultant: Brad Tennant, PhD,
Associate Professor of History, Presentation
College

All rights reserved. International copyright
secured. No part of this book may be
reproduced, stored in a retrieval system, or
transmitted in any form or by any means—
electronic, mechanical, photocopying,
recording, or otherwise—without the prior
written permission of Lerner Publishing
Group, Inc., except for the inclusion of brief
quotations in an acknowledged review.

Lerner Publications Company
A division of Lerner Publishing Group, Inc.
241 First Avenue North
Minneapolis, MN 55401 USA

For reading levels and more information, look
up this title at www.lernerbooks.com.

Main body text set in ITC Franklin Gothic Std
Book Condensed 12/15.
Typeface provided by Adobe Systems.

Library of Congress Cataloging-in-Publication
Data

Meinking, Mary.
    What's great about South Dakota? / by
Mary Meinking.
        pages   cm. — (Our great states)
    Includes index.
    Audience: Ages 7–11.
    ISBN 978-1-4677-3869-9 (lib. bdg. :
alk. paper) — ISBN 978-1-4677-6093-5
(pbk.) — ISBN 978-1-4677-6271-7 (EB pdf)
        1. South Dakota--Juvenile literature.
I. Title.
F651.3.M45 2015
978.3—dc23   2014028749

Manufactured in the United States of America
1 - PC – 12/31/14

SOUTH DAKOTA Welcomes You!

South Dakota has a lot to offer. It has grassy prairies and stunning rock formations in the Black Hills. You can even explore underground caves. Learn more about South Dakota's history at the Mammoth Site. Here you'll see fossils of animals that lived thousands of years ago. Or maybe you'd like to learn more about the gold rush at Broken Boot Gold Mine. Experience pioneer life at the Ingalls Homestead. There is something for everyone to explore in South Dakota. Turn the page to find out more about what makes this state great!

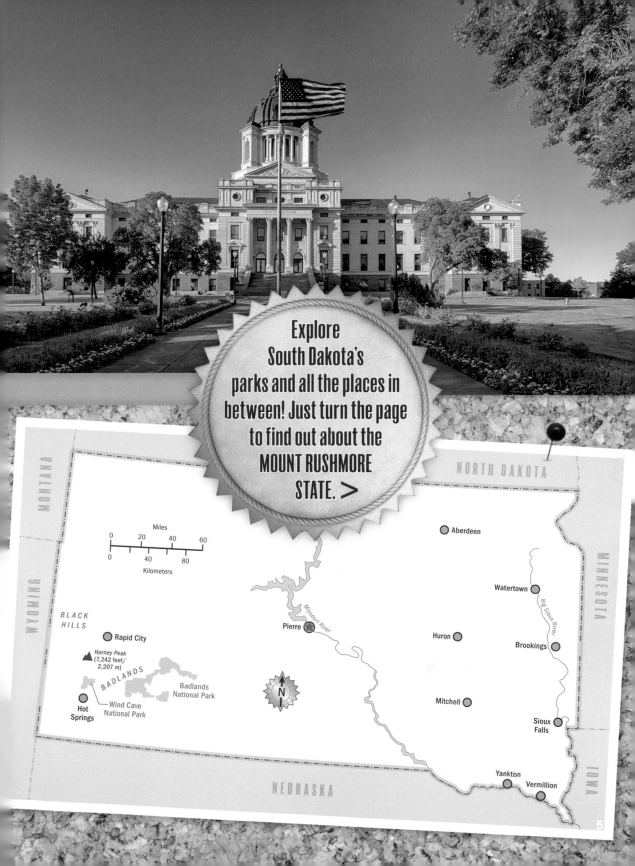

Explore
South Dakota's
parks and all the places in
between! Just turn the page
to find out about the
MOUNT RUSHMORE
STATE. >

MONTANA

WYOMING

NORTH DAKOTA

MINNESOTA

IOWA

NEBRASKA

Miles
0   20   40   60
0   40   80
Kilometers

BLACK
HILLS

● Rapid City

▲ Harney Peak
(7,242 feet/
2,207 m)

BADLANDS

Badlands
National Park

Wind Cave
National Park

● Hot
Springs

Missouri River

● Pierre

N

● Aberdeen

Watertown ●

Big Sioux River

Huron ●

Brookings ●

Mitchell ●

Sioux
Falls ●

Yankton ●   Vermillion ●

MOUNT RUSHMORE NATIONAL MEMORIAL

> No trip to South Dakota is complete without a stop at the Mount Rushmore National Memorial near Keystone. Here you'll see the faces of US presidents George Washington, Thomas Jefferson, Theodore Roosevelt, and Abraham Lincoln carved into granite. Mount Rushmore is one of the most recognized American symbols.

Make your first stop the visitor center. You can walk through exhibits. You'll see original tools from when the carving first started in 1927. Or you can watch a short movie about carving Mount Rushmore. Once you're done, head outside. Then hike the Presidential Trail. This will take you close to the mountain. You may see frogs or Rocky Mountain goats on your walk.

If you're visiting Mount Rushmore in the summer, stop at the Lakota, Nakota, and Dakota Heritage Village. Here you'll learn about American Indians living in South Dakota. A lighting ceremony at the monument takes place in the summer at dusk. This program includes a short talk, a video, and a flag ceremony. Then the presidents' faces are lit up.

Learn about American Indian teepees at the Lakota, Nakota, and Dakota Heritage Village.

BADLANDS NATIONAL PARK

> Continue your South Dakota journey at Badlands National Park in the southwestern part of the state. Here, cool rock formations, fossils, and wildlife surround you. There are more than 244,000 acres (98,743 hectares) to explore!

Start your tour at the visitor center. You can watch a video about the rock formations and touch fossilized animals. You can also put together a skeleton on the computer. Sign up for a ranger-led hike. Or maybe you'd like to take a ride with your family on the Badlands Loop Road. You can drive around the entire park. Be on the lookout for wildlife such as bison and bobcats.

On your drive, stop and walk the Fossil Exhibit Trail. You'll see fossil replicas of animals that used to live in the area. Then stop at Roberts Prairie Dog Town on the east side of the park. This area is home to many prairie dogs.

You can buy a bag of peanuts to feed the prairie dogs at Roberts Prairie Dog Town.

LAND FORMATIONS

South Dakota has many land formations. Thousands of years ago, glaciers flattened the eastern half of the state. The Black Hills hug the western border of South Dakota. Their granite peaks look like smaller versions of the Rocky Mountains. The Black Hills are the oldest mountains in the United States. The Badlands rise out of the prairie in the southwestern part of the state. They were created from millions of years of wind and water erosion.

CUSTER STATE PARK

> Experience the outdoors at Custer State Park in Custer. This park is one of the largest state parks in the country. There is so much to do here! There are several scenic drives in the park. If you'd like to see animals up close, take the 18-mile (29 kilometer) Wildlife Loop. Sunrise and sunset are when you'll see the most animals. A herd of more than thirteen hundred bison live in the park. They roam free and sometimes stop traffic by standing in the road. You may also see burros, elk, coyotes, prairie dogs, mountain goats, and bighorn sheep.

After driving around the park, stretch your legs and attend a ranger-led program. Maybe you'd like to try panning for gold. Or you can learn how to fish for trout. There is a program for everyone.

You'll feel like a real cowpoke when you go on the Blue Bell Hayride and Chuck Wagon Cookout. Join in the sing-along and eat cowboy food.

Take home your cowboy hat and bandana after the Chuck Wagon Cookout.

Some animals in Custer State Park, including burros, come to car windows looking for treats.

SOUTH DAKOTA'S CAVES

> Continue your visit of Custer belowground at the Jewel Cave National Monument. Grab your sweatshirt to explore the maze of caves. It can be chilly belowground.

Jewel Cave is the third-longest cave in the world. It has more than 170 miles (274 km) of mapped cave paths. Join one of several ranger-led tours. The Historic Lantern Tour transports you back to the 1930s. The only light on this tour comes from your group's lanterns. Listen as your ranger points out rock formations on the Discovery Tour.

After touring Jewel Cave, hop in the car for a one-hour trip east. Here you can explore Wind Cave National Park in Hot Springs. Sign up for a cave tour. While you wait for your tour, walk through the visitor center. Learn more about cave formations and early cave history. You can also enjoy a short movie about Wind Cave. This cave is sacred to the Sioux American Indians.

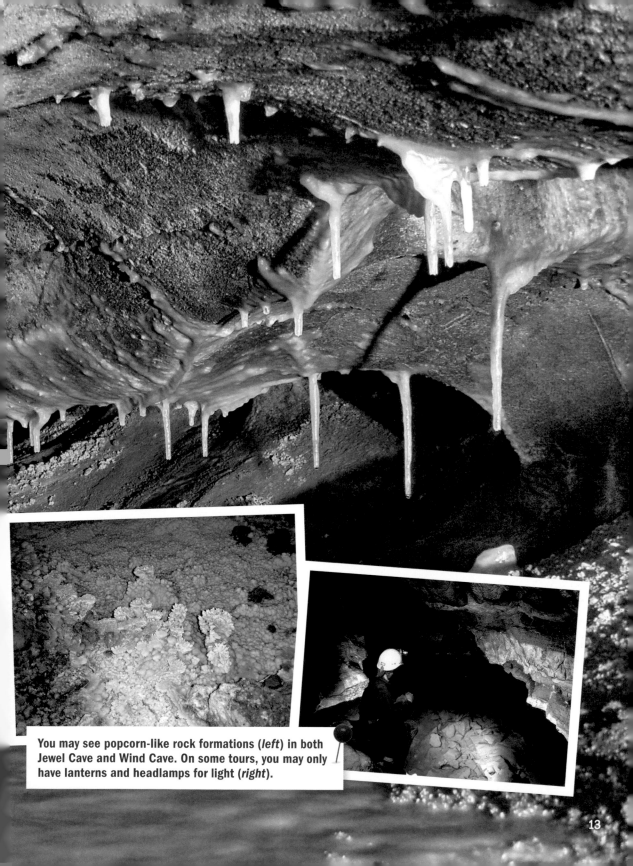

You may see popcorn-like rock formations (*left*) in both Jewel Cave and Wind Cave. On some tours, you may only have lanterns and headlamps for light (*right*).

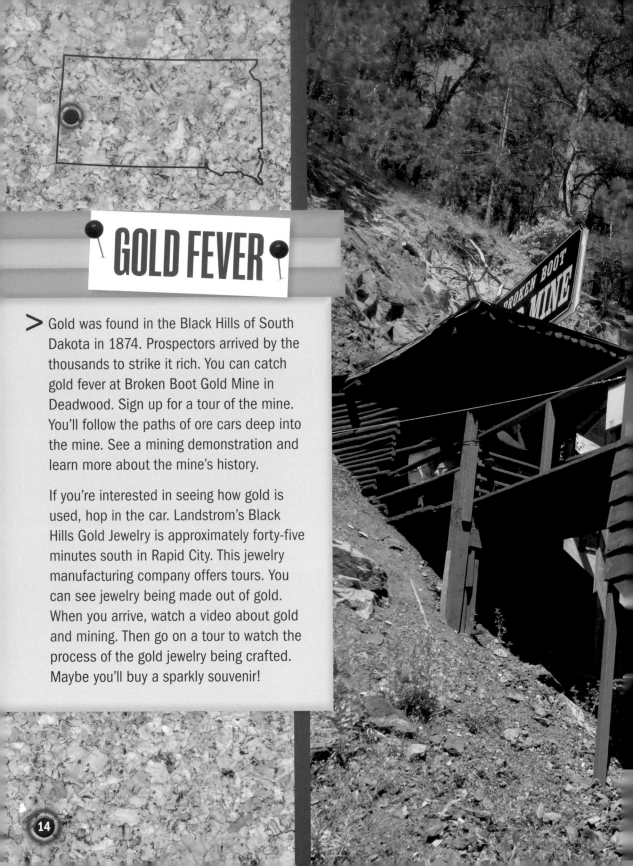

GOLD FEVER

> Gold was found in the Black Hills of South Dakota in 1874. Prospectors arrived by the thousands to strike it rich. You can catch gold fever at Broken Boot Gold Mine in Deadwood. Sign up for a tour of the mine. You'll follow the paths of ore cars deep into the mine. See a mining demonstration and learn more about the mine's history.

If you're interested in seeing how gold is used, hop in the car. Landstrom's Black Hills Gold Jewelry is approximately forty-five minutes south in Rapid City. This jewelry manufacturing company offers tours. You can see jewelry being made out of gold. When you arrive, watch a video about gold and mining. Then go on a tour to watch the process of the gold jewelry being crafted. Maybe you'll buy a sparkly souvenir!

Once you've finished your tour at Broken Boot Gold Mine, try panning for gold.

THE BLACK HILLS

The Sioux American Indians have lived in South Dakota since the early 1700s. By the 1800s, Europeans moved into the territory. This caused many conflicts. A treaty in 1868 set aside land for the Sioux. This included the Black Hills. But in 1874, gold was discovered in the Black Hills. Word quickly spread, and more than ten thousand prospectors rushed to the area. The US government attempted to buy the area from the Sioux. The Sioux refused to sell. The Black Hills continues to be a sacred place for the Sioux.

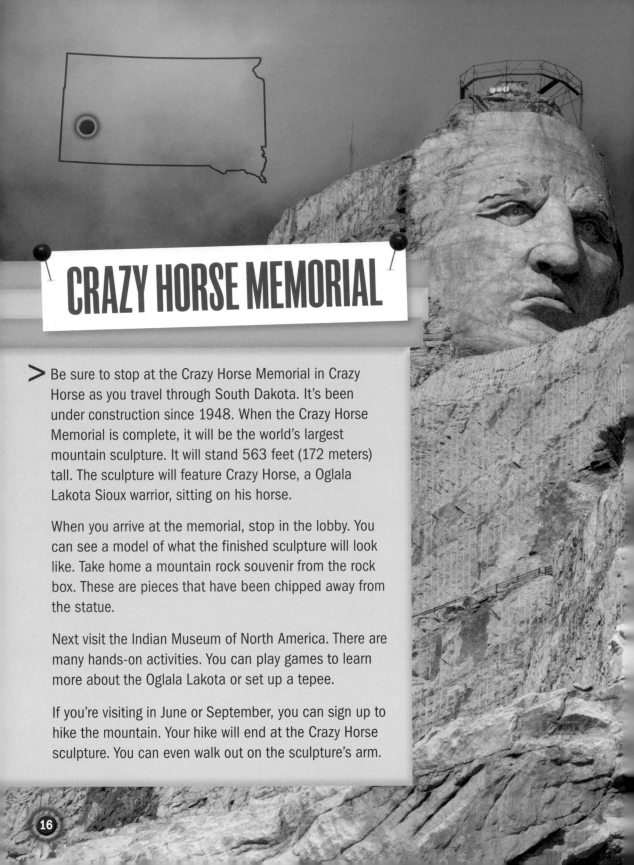

CRAZY HORSE MEMORIAL

> Be sure to stop at the Crazy Horse Memorial in Crazy Horse as you travel through South Dakota. It's been under construction since 1948. When the Crazy Horse Memorial is complete, it will be the world's largest mountain sculpture. It will stand 563 feet (172 meters) tall. The sculpture will feature Crazy Horse, a Oglala Lakota Sioux warrior, sitting on his horse.

When you arrive at the memorial, stop in the lobby. You can see a model of what the finished sculpture will look like. Take home a mountain rock souvenir from the rock box. These are pieces that have been chipped away from the statue.

Next visit the Indian Museum of North America. There are many hands-on activities. You can play games to learn more about the Oglala Lakota or set up a tepee.

If you're visiting in June or September, you can sign up to hike the mountain. Your hike will end at the Crazy Horse sculpture. You can even walk out on the sculpture's arm.

You can walk inside a tepee at the Indian Museum of North America. Some American Indians lived in these cone-shaped homes in the past.

FAMOUS SIOUX CHIEFS

Chiefs Sitting Bull and Crazy Horse led the Sioux to fight for their land in the 1800s. They defeated Lieutenant Colonel George Armstrong Custer and his troops in 1876 at the Battle of the Little Bighorn in Montana.

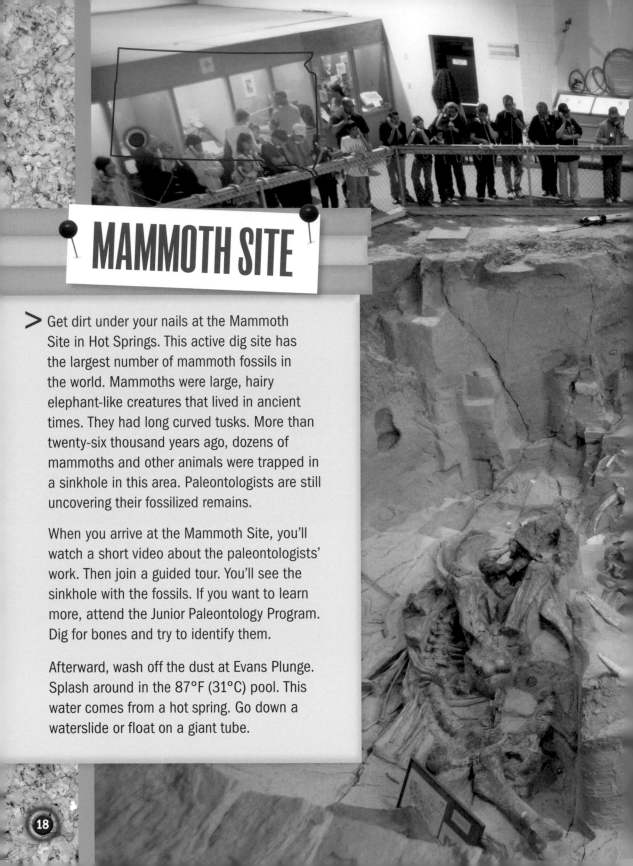

MAMMOTH SITE

> Get dirt under your nails at the Mammoth Site in Hot Springs. This active dig site has the largest number of mammoth fossils in the world. Mammoths were large, hairy elephant-like creatures that lived in ancient times. They had long curved tusks. More than twenty-six thousand years ago, dozens of mammoths and other animals were trapped in a sinkhole in this area. Paleontologists are still uncovering their fossilized remains.

When you arrive at the Mammoth Site, you'll watch a short video about the paleontologists' work. Then join a guided tour. You'll see the sinkhole with the fossils. If you want to learn more, attend the Junior Paleontology Program. Dig for bones and try to identify them.

Afterward, wash off the dust at Evans Plunge. Splash around in the 87°F (31°C) pool. This water comes from a hot spring. Go down a waterslide or float on a giant tube.

See how huts were built during the Ice Age in one of Mammoth Site's exhibits (*left*). You can also see life-size replicas of the mammoths at Mammoth Site (*right*).

CHILDREN'S MUSEUM

> For hours of fun, stop at the Children's Museum of South Dakota in Brookings. You can explore many hands-on exhibits. Start your visit in the Our Prairie exhibit. You'll learn about pioneers and farming. Climb a cloud jungle gym to discover more about wind and weather.

Try out different jobs on Kidstreet. You can make a sandwich at the café. Or maybe you'd like to create a TV show. At the post office, you can weigh packages and sort mail. Then practice daily chores on the prairie. You can sort vegetables and fruit in the grocery store.

Make your way to the outdoor exhibits. You can climb logs or make mud pies. Help build a beaver dam. Then fish in the pond. End your visit digging up dinosaur bones. Wave hi to Mama, an animated 25-foot-tall (8 m) *Tyrannosaurus rex*.

Pioneers helped build South Dakota into the state it is today. Learn more about pioneers at the Children's Museum.

INGALLS HOMESTEAD

> Step back in time at the Ingalls Homestead in De Smet. Famous author Laura Ingalls Wilder and her family settled in the area in the late 1800s.

Take a covered wagon tour of the prairie. Your driver will tell you about the history of the area. Then visit the Little Prairie School. Try on a bonnet or a straw hat as you sit in the one-room schoolhouse. Listen to a short lesson from the schoolteacher.

Help out with some chores on the farm. Learn to make rope or grind wheat. You can also twist hay to burn in the stove. The hay helped keep pioneers' houses warm in the winter. Walk through the cottonwood grove that Pa Ingalls planted.

If you're visiting in June or July, you might catch the Laura Ingalls Wilder Pageant. It is held for three weeks each year. Hop aboard a covered wagon, or help pump water from the well.

The original Ingalls house and barn have been rebuilt for visitors to see.

LAURA INGALLS WILDER

Laura Ingalls Wilder was a famous South Dakota writer. She arrived in the Dakota Territory with her family in the late 1880s. They came there to farm. Laura went on to write many books, including the Little House series. She wrote two books, *The Long Winter* and *The Little Town on the Prairie*, that were set in De Smet. The books tell of experiences that her family and many pioneers had in South Dakota.

SIOUX FALLS

> End your visit of South Dakota in its largest city, Sioux Falls. Spend the morning exploring the Kirby Science Discovery Center. There are more than one hundred exhibits to see. Fly a space shuttle or dig up a dinosaur. In one exhibit, you can feel what it's like to be inside a tornado. Help build a race car before visiting the center's live beehive. Next, climb as high as you can on the rock wall. Then make some music on the giant piano on the floor.

Head across town to the Sertoma Butterfly House & Marine Cove. It is home to nearly one thousand butterflies from many continents. Wear bright-colored clothing. This will encourage the fluttering butterflies to land on you.

The Marine Cove is home to thirteen aquariums. Keep your eyes open for coral, clown fish, and stingrays. You may even see a shark!

Stingrays arc just one of the animals you'll see at Sertoma Butterfly House & Marine Cove.

YOUR TOP TEN!

You've just read about ten awesome things to see and do in South Dakota. Now it's your turn! If you visited South Dakota, what would be on your Top Ten list? What places in South Dakota do you really want to visit? Grab a sheet of paper and jot down your South Dakota Top Ten list. You could even make it into a book, complete with your own drawings or pictures from the Internet.

SOUTH DAKOTA BY MAP

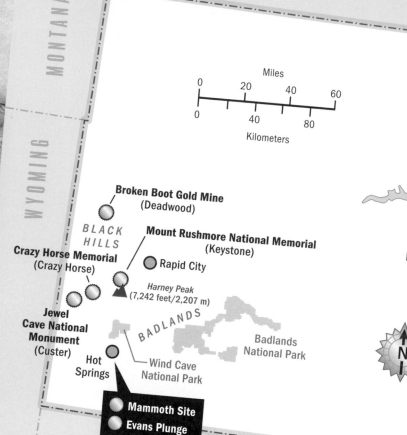

MONTANA

WYOMING

Miles
0   20   40   60

0   40   80
Kilometers

Broken Boot Gold Mine
(Deadwood)

B L A C K
HILLS

Mount Rushmore National Memorial
(Keystone)

Crazy Horse Memorial
(Crazy Horse)

Rapid City

Harney Peak
(7,242 feet/2,207 m)

**Jewel
Cave National
Monument**
(Custer)

B A D L A N D S

Badlands
National Park

Hot
Springs

Wind Cave
National Park

N

Mammoth Site
Evans Plunge

Pierre

Missouri River

NEBRASKA

⭐ Capital city

⭕ City

◯ Point of interest

▲ Highest elevation

–··– State border

NORTH DAKOTA

MINNESOTA

◯ Aberdeen

Watertown ⭕

Children's Museum of South Dakota

Big Sioux River

Huron ⭕

Ingalls Homestead (De Smet)

⭕ Brookings

Mitchell ⭕

Sioux Falls ⭕

Sertoma Butterfly House & Marine Cove

Kirby Science Discovery Center

Yankton ⭕

Vermillion ⭕

IOWA

Visit www.lernerresource.com to learn more about the state flag of South Dakota.

SOUTH DAKOTA FACTS

NICKNAME: The Mount Rushmore State

SONG: "Hail! South Dakota" by DeeCort Hammitt

MOTTO: "Under God the People Rule"

> **FLOWER:** American pasque flower

TREE: Black Hills spruce

> **BIRD:** Chinese ring-necked pheasant

ANIMAL: coyote

FOODS: kuchen (German word for "cake")

DATE AND RANK OF STATEHOOD: November 2, 1889; the 40th state

> **CAPITAL:** Pierre

AREA: 77,116 square miles (199,730 sq. km)

AVERAGE JANUARY TEMPERATURE: 16°F (-9°C)

AVERAGE JULY TEMPERATURE: 74°F (23°C)

POPULATION AND RANK: 844,877; 46th (2013)

MAJOR CITIES AND POPULATIONS: Sioux Falls (164,676), Rapid City (70,812), Aberdeen (27,333), Brookings (22,943), Watertown (21,995)

NUMBER OF US CONGRESS MEMBERS: 1 representative, 2 senators

NUMBER OF ELECTORAL VOTES: 3

NATURAL RESOURCES: gold, beryl, feldspar, mica, silver, uranium

> **AGRICULTURAL PRODUCTS:** beef cattle, corn, hay, hogs, milk, turkeys

MANUFACTURED GOODS: chemicals, computer and electronic products, food products, machinery, transportation equipment, gold jewelery

STATE HOLIDAYS AND CELEBRATIONS: Laura Ingalls Wilder Pageant, Native American Day

GLOSSARY

erosion: the gradual destruction of something by natural forces

exhibit: a collection of objects put in a public space for people to look at

glacier: a large area of ice that moves slowly down a slope or valley

homestead: a piece of government land that a person could get by living and farming on it

manufacturing: the process of making products, especially with machines, in factories

paleontologist: a scientist who studies fossils of plants and animals of the past

pioneer: someone who is one of the first people to move to and live in an area

prospector: a person in search of gold, minerals, or other valuable resources

replica: an exact or very close copy of something

souvenir: something that is kept as a reminder of a place you have visited

LERNER

Expand learning beyond the printed book. Download free, complementary educational resources for this book from our website, www.lerneresource.com.

SOURCE

FURTHER INFORMATION

Badlands National Park
http://www.nps.gov/badl/forkids/parkfun.htm
Learn about animal tracks and constellations, make an armored mud ball, try fossil puzzles and the Geology Challenge, and have a virtual experience of the Badlands.

Glaser, Jason. *South Dakota: The Mount Rushmore State*. New York: PowerKids, 2010. Learn more about South Dakota's geography and places to visit in this book.

Hunhoff, Bernie. *South Dakota Curiosities: Quirky Characters, Roadside Oddities, and Other Offbeat Stuff*. Guilford, CT: Globe Pequot, 2007. This book covers the interesting and quirky side of South Dakota.

Jango-Cohen, Judith. *Mount Rushmore*. Minneapolis: Lerner Publications, 2011. Photos, illustrations, and fast facts help you learn more about one of South Dakota's most popular attractions.

Mount Rushmore National Memorial
http://www.nps.gov/moru/forkids/kids-fun-page.htm
Do word searches, word scrambles, and crossword puzzles, and learn more about the presidents.

South Dakota State Historical Society
http://www.sd4history.com
This website has many history lessons on South Dakota. Learn something new or read more about a sight mentioned in this book.

INDEX

PHOTO ACKNOWLEDGMENTS

The images in this book are used with the permission of: © welcomia/Shutterstock Images, p. 1; NASA, pp. 2–3; © Tom Reichner/Shutterstock Images, pp. 4, 29 (bottom left); © Nagel Photography/Shutterstock Images, p. 5 (top); © Laura Westlund/Independent Picture Service, pp. 5 (bottom), 26–27; National Park Service, pp. 6–7, 8–9, 9, 12–13, 13; © Melanie Stetson Freeman/The Christian Science Monitor/AP Images, p. 7; © turtix/Shutterstock Images, pp. 10–11; © Danita Delimont/Alamy, p. 11 (left); © Wollertz/Shutterstock Images, p. 11 (right); © Don Smetzer/Shutterstock Images, pp. 14–15; © Robert Gubbins/Shutterstock Images, p. 15 (top); © Zack Frank/Shutterstock Images, p. 15 (bottom); © Sergio Pitamitz/Danita Delimont Photography/Newscom, pp. 16–17; © David R. Frazier Photolibrary, Inc./Alamy, p. 17 (top); Public Domain, pp. 17 (bottom), 23 (bottom); © Michael Snell/Robert Harding/Newscom, pp. 18–19; © Wiskerke/Alamy, p. 19 (left); © Blaine Harrington III/Alamy, p. 19 (right); © chromographs/Shutterstock Images, pp. 20–21; Library of Congress, p. 21 (LC-USZ62-13655); © Beth Gauper/KRT/Newscom, pp. 22–23, 23 (top); © Michael Warwick/Shutterstock Images, pp. 24–25; © Kristina Vackova/Shutterstock Images, p. 25 (top); © Dirk Lammers/AP Images, p. 25 (bottom); © Globe Turner/Shutterstock Images, p. 27; © Holly Kuchera/Shutterstock Images, p. 29 (top right); © Arto Hakola/Shutterstock Images, p. 29 (top left); © dustin77a/Shutterstock Images, p. 29 (bottom right).

Cover: © Ron Chapple/Dreamstime.com (Mt. Rushmore); South Dakota Department of Tourism (Powwow); © iStockphoto.com/worldofphotos (Badlands); © Laura Westlund/Independent Picture Service (map); © iStockphoto.com/fpm (seal); © iStockphoto.com/vicm (pushpins); © iStockphoto.com/benz190 (cork board).